Contents

W9-CPA-187

Emergency! — page 4

Wheels, Engines, and Buttons — page 9

EMTs — page 12

Saving Lives — page 18

Ambulance Diagram — page 28

Fun Facts — page 29

Glossary — page 30

Further Reading — page 31

Index — page 32

Emergency!

Move over, cars!
Something speedy is
on the road.
What is it?

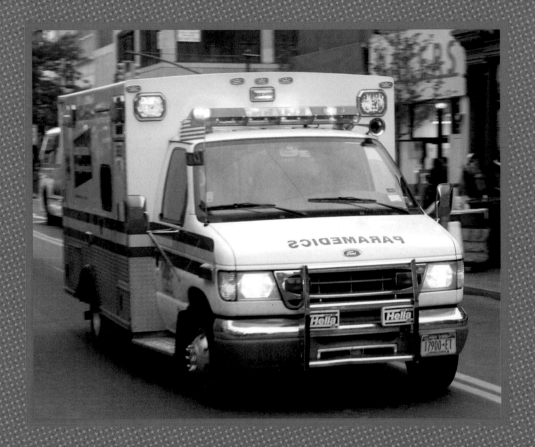

LIGHTNING
BOLT
BOOKS™

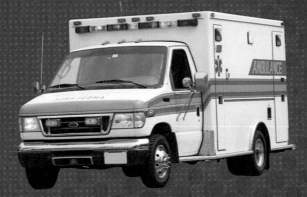

Ambulances
on the Move

Laura Hamilton Waxman

Lerner Publications
Minneapolis

Lerner Publications Company
A division of Lerner Publishing Group, Inc.
241 First Avenue North
Minneapolis, MN 55401 USA

For reading levels and more information, look up this title at www.lernerbooks.com.

Library of Congress Cataloging-in-Publication Data

Waxman, Laura Hamilton.
    Ambulances on the move / by Laura Hamilton Waxman.
        p.   cm. — (Lightning bolt books™ — Vroom-vroom)
    Includes index.
    ISBN 978-0-7613-3922-9 (lib. bdg. : alk. paper)
    ISBN 978-0-7613-7230-1 (eb pdf)
    1. Ambulances—Juvenile literature. 2. Emergency medicine—Juvenile literature. I. Title.
    TL235.8.W39 2011
    629.222'34—dc22   2009043793

Manufactured in the United States of America
2-42836-10064-8/16/2016

An ambulance zooms past cars on a busy city street.

This is an ambulance.

Ambulances rush to emergencies. They take sick or hurt people to the hospital.

This ambulance is in a hurry.

Bright lights flash. Loud sirens howl. WHEE-OOO! What are the lights and the sirens for?

Lights flash as this ambulance speeds through the night.

The lights and the sirens warn drivers that an ambulance is coming. Cars must pull over to let it by.

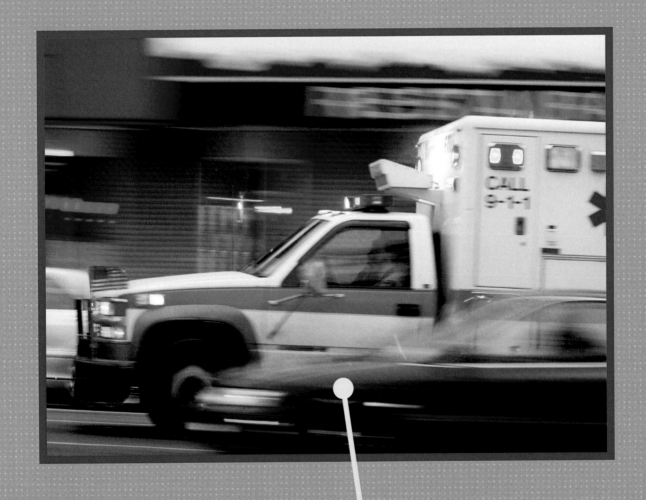

A car moves out of the way so an ambulance can pass.

Wheels, Engines, and Buttons

Four wheels take the ambulance to an emergency. An engine gives the wheels power.

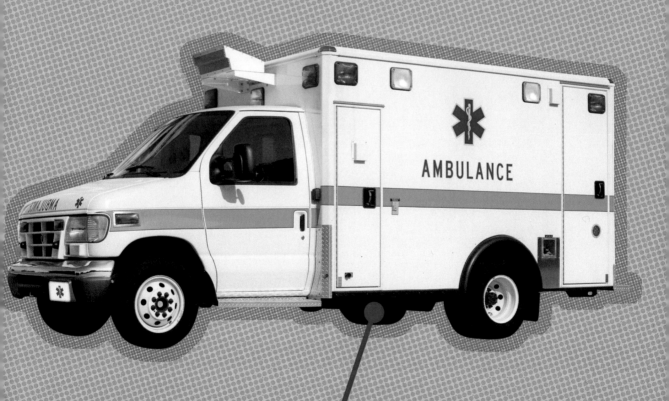

All ambulances have four wheels.

The front of the ambulance is where the driver sits.

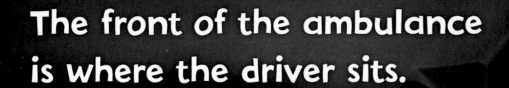

An ambulance driver talks on his radio as he drives.

Inside, the driver pushes buttons. The buttons turn the ambulance's lights and sirens on or off.

Buttons for the lights and sirens are within easy reach.

EMTs

EMTs ride in the back of the ambulance. EMTs are emergency medical technicians.

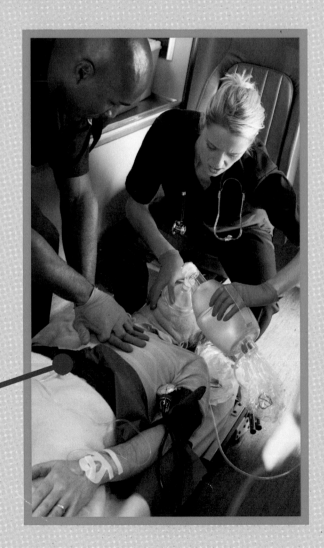

EMTs help an injured person in the back of an ambulance.

EMTs use special equipment to help sick or hurt people. Where do EMTs keep their equipment?

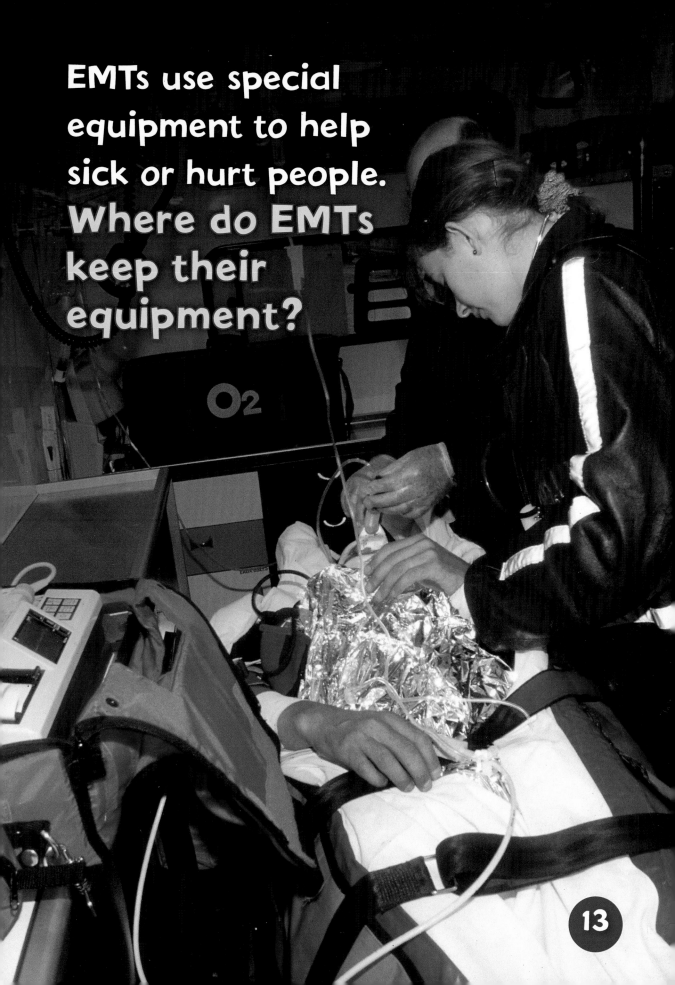

Many cabinets are in the back of the ambulance.

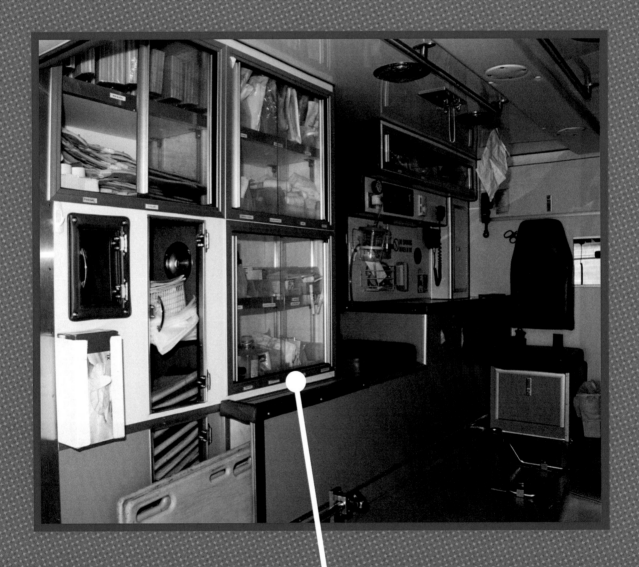

Cabinets line the walls inside this ambulance.

The cabinets store
some of the equipment
for EMTs.

Doors on the outside of the ambulance open.

More equipment is stored behind them.

A stretcher is stored behind this door.

Saving Lives

This ambulance has arrived at an emergency.

EMTs carry the patient into the back of the ambulance. Wide doors let the patient through.

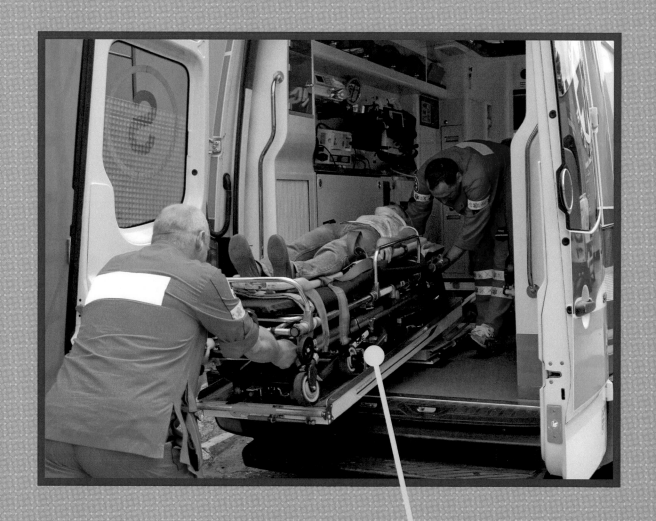

Two EMTs put a patient into the back of an ambulance.

The back of the ambulance
has room for the patient and
the EMTs.

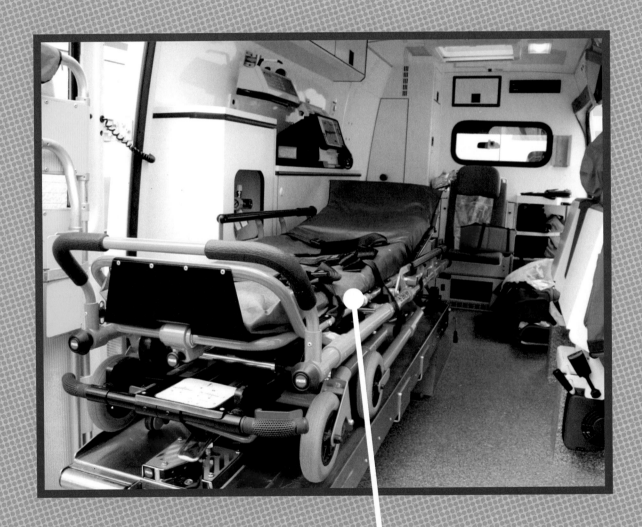

Patients ride on stretchers
like this one in the back of
an ambulance.

EMTs sit near the patient on chairs and benches. They take care of the patient on the way to the hospital.

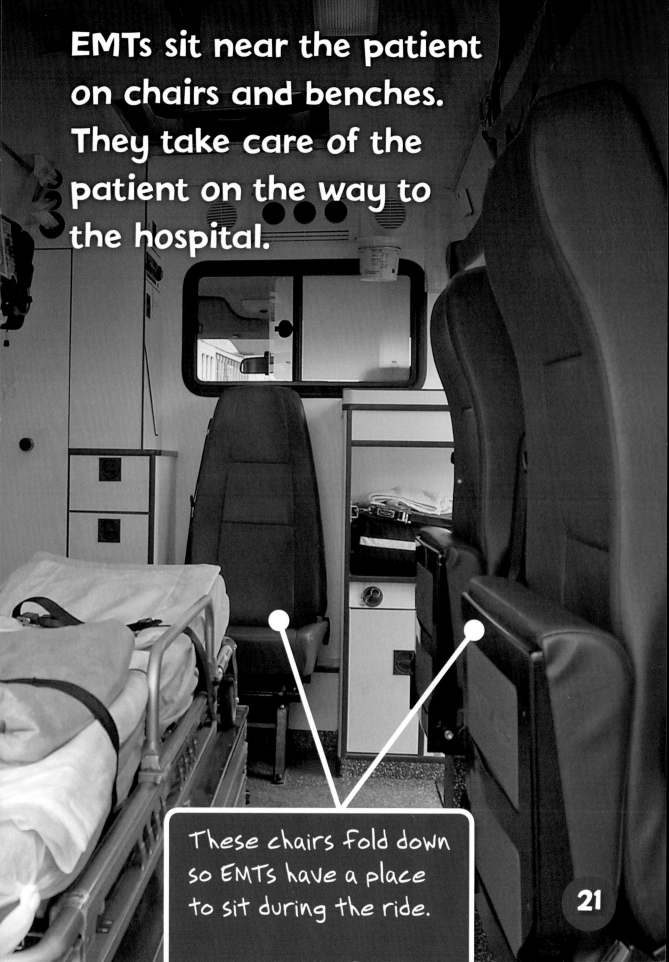

These chairs fold down so EMTs have a place to sit during the ride.

This ambulance has arrived at a hospital.

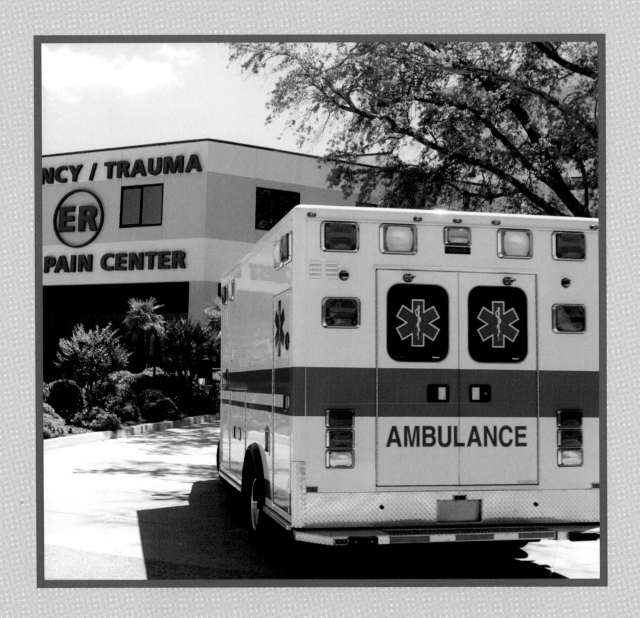

What happens next?

EMTs rush the patient inside.
The ambulance's work is done.

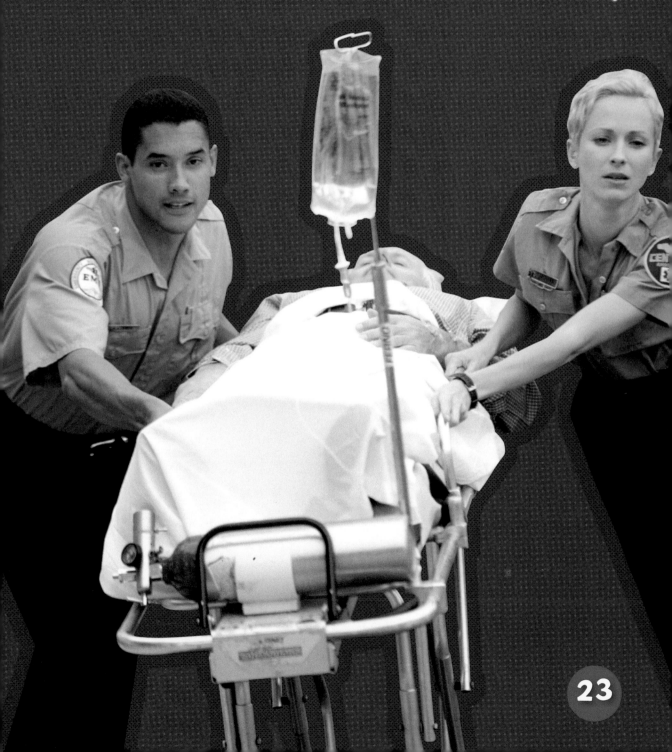

This ambulance is

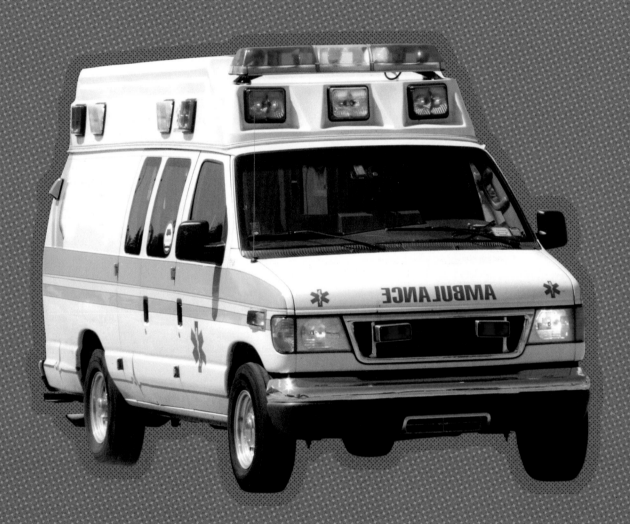

on its way home.

Some ambulances stay at hospitals. Other ambulances belong to fire departments or police stations.

Two ambulances stay at this firehouse.

But all ambulances
do the same job.

They help save lives!

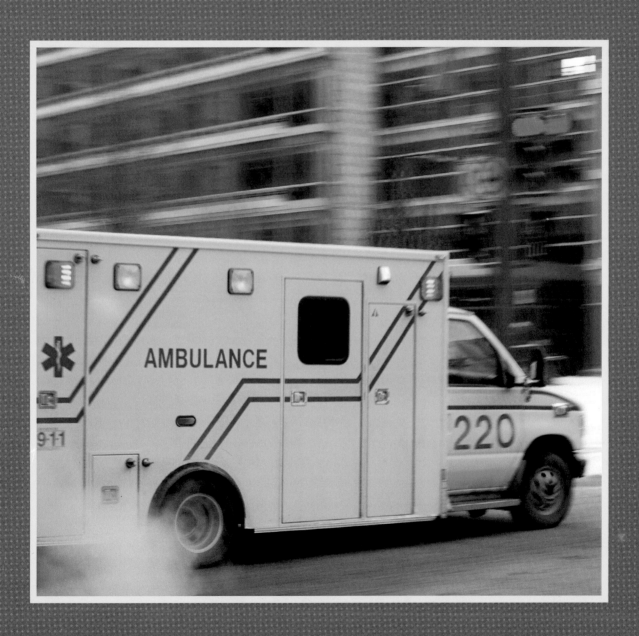

Ambulance Diagram

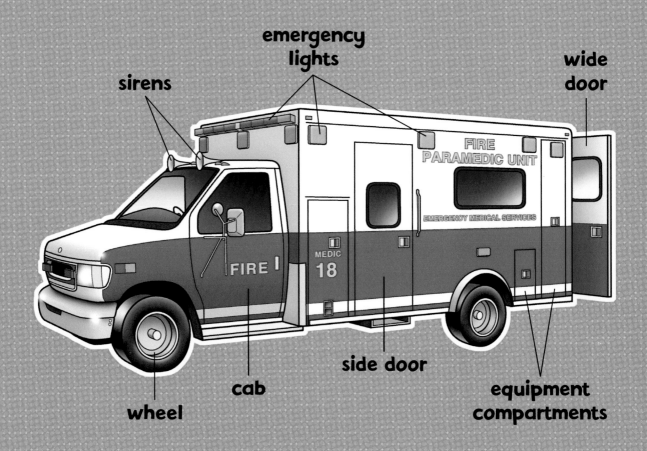

emergency
lights

sirens

wide
door

FIRE
PARAMEDIC UNIT

EMERGENCY MEDICAL SERVICES

FIRE

MEDIC
18

side door

cab

wheel

equipment
compartments

Fun Facts

- Most ambulances are either vans or trucks that are specially made to do their job.

- Sometimes airplanes and helicopters are used as ambulances. Airplanes and helicopters can travel much more quickly than trucks. And airplanes and helicopters can get to places that trucks cannot.

- The word *ambulance* is written backward on some ambulances. That's because drivers often use rearview mirrors in their cars to see other traffic on the road. Backward writing looks normal when you see it in a mirror.

- Most ambulances have a telephone in the back of the ambulance. That way, EMTs can talk to doctors and nurses on the way to the hospital.

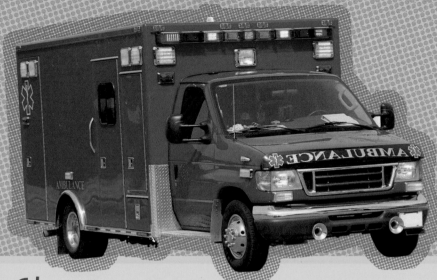

Glossary

cabinet: a place to store things. Most cabinets have shelves and doors.

emergency: a serious problem, such as a bad accident or an illness

EMT: an emergency medical technician. EMTs help sick or hurt people in emergencies.

engine: the part of an ambulance that gives it the power to move

equipment: tools used to help sick or hurt people

patient: a person who is sick or hurt and needs to go to the hospital

siren: the part of an ambulance that makes loud warning sounds

Further Reading

Amoroso, Gary M. *Ambulances.* Chanhassen, MN: Child's World, 2007.

Brecke, Nicole, and Patricia M. Stockland. *Cars, Trucks, and Motorcycles You Can Draw.* Minneapolis: Millbrook Press, 2010.

Enchanted Learning: Vehicle Online Coloring Pages http://www.enchantedlearning.com/vehicles/ paintonline.shtml

Jango-Cohen, Judith. *Fire Trucks on the Move.* Minneapolis: Lerner Publications Company, 2011.

Manolis, Kay. *Ambulances.* Minneapolis: Bellwether Media, 2008.

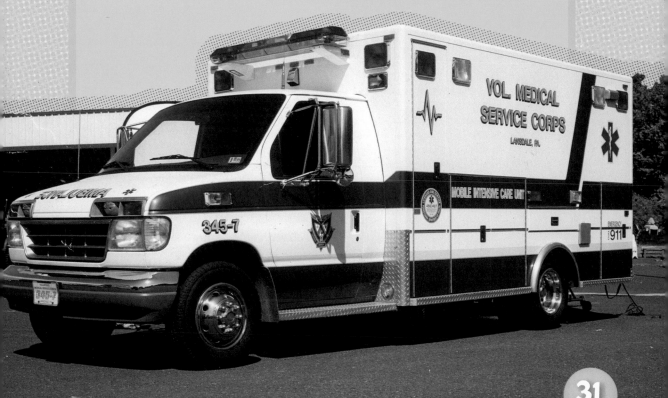

Index

cabinets, 14–15

doors, 16–17, 19, 28

EMTs (emergency
  medical technicians),
  12–13, 15, 19–21, 23, 29
equipment, 13, 15, 17, 28

lights, 7–8, 11, 28

patient, 19–21, 23

sirens, 7–8, 11, 28

wheels, 9, 28

Photo Acknowledgments

The images in this book are used with the permission of: © Travis Manley/Dreamstime.com, p. 1; © Comstock Images/Getty Images, p. 2; © Transtock/SuperStock, p. 4; © age fotostock/SuperStock, pp. 5, 8; © Luckynick/Dreamstime.com, p. 6; © Ramon Berk/Dreamstime.com, p. 7; © Robwilson39/Dreamstime.com, p. 9; © Lisette Le Bon/SuperStock, pp. 10, 11; © Monkey Business Images/Dreamstime.com, p. 12; © Photononstop/SuperStock, p. 13; © Morey Milbradt/Brand X Pictures/Getty Images, p. 14; © Tanja Rosso/Dreamstime.com, p. 15; © Todd Strand/Independent Picture Service, pp. 16, 17; © Les Palenik/Dreamstime.com, p. 18; © Pawel Nawrot/Dreamstime.com, p. 19; © Marekp/Dreamstime.com, p. 20; © Rorem/Dreamstime.com, p. 21; © Steven Frame/Dreamstime.com, p. 22; © Kwame Zikomo/SuperStock, p. 23; © Robert Asento/Dreamstime.com, p. 24; © Adam Jones/The Image Bank/Getty Images, p. 25; © Bob Peterson/UpperCut Images/Getty Images, p. 26; © Flaviu Boerescu/Dreamstime.com, p. 27; © Laura Westlund/Independent Picture Service, p. 28; © Carlos Santa Maria/Dreamstime.com, p. 30; © Richard Leeney/Dorling Kindersley/Getty Images, p. 31.

Front cover: © Robert Pernell/Shutterstock Images (top); © Comstock Images/Getty Images (bottom).